OVERCOMING ANXIETY

Effective Solutions To A Growing Problem

Lynn Fossum

A FIFTY-MINUTE™ SERIES BOOK

CRISP PUBLICATIONS, INC.
Menlo Park, California

OVERCOMING ANXIETY
Effective Solutions To
A Growing Problem

Lynn Fossum

CREDITS
Editor: **Michael Crisp**
Designer: **Carol Harris**
Layout and Composition: **Interface Studio**
Cover Design: **Carol Harris**
Artwork: **Ralph Mapson**

Copyright © 1990 by Crisp Publications, Inc.
Printed in the United States of America

English language Crisp books are distributed worldwide. Our major international distributors include:

CANADA: Reid Publishing Ltd., Box 69559—109 Thomas St., Oakville, Ontario, Canada L6J 7R4. TEL: (905) 842-4428, FAX: (905) 842-9327

Raincoast Books Distribution Ltd., 112 East 3rd Avenue, Vancouver, British Columbia, Canada V5T 1C8. TEL: (604) 873-6581, FAX: (604) 874-2711

AUSTRALIA: Career Builders, P.O. Box 1051, Springwood, Brisbane, Queensland, Australia 4127. TEL: 841-1061, FAX: 841-1580

NEW ZEALAND: Career Builders, P.O. Box 571, Manurewa, Auckland, New Zealand. TEL: 266-5276, FAX: 266-4152

JAPAN: Phoenix Associates Co., Mizuho Bldg. 2-12-2, Kami Osaki, Shinagawa-Ku, Tokyo 141, Japan. TEL: 3-443-7231, FAX: 3-443-7640

Selected Crisp titles are also available in other languages. Contact International Rights Manager Suzanne Kelly at (415) 323-6100 for more information.

Library of Congress Catalog Card Number 89-82051
Fossum, Lynn
Overcoming Anxiety
ISBN 1-56052-029-9

This book is printed on recyclable paper with soy ink.

PREFACE

Are you sensing a vague feeling of uneasiness, tension and apprehension in facing today's world? If so, you are not alone.

Anxiety is becoming a major clinical issue. More and more people are seeking professional assistance for anxiety-related disorders. Xanax (an anti-anxiety medication) has exceeded Valium (a tranquilizer) as the most frequently prescribed drug for psychological difficulties.

You may be feeling a sense of anxiety about your job, your lifestyle, natural disasters or even the threat of nuclear war. OVERCOMING ANXIETY gives you a clearer understanding about uncomfortable feelings and physical symptoms. More importantly, it provides effective techniques that you can apply immediately to help cope with today's problems.

Please note that the ideas, techniques and suggestions in this book are not intended to be a substitute for competent medical advice or psychotherapy. You should have regular, thorough physical examinations and consult with your physician on any matters regarding your health and well-being. There are some illnesses that mimic anxiety or increase your body's physiological anxiety responses. Therefore, if severe anxiety continues to be a difficulty for you, consult your physician. Seeking the assistance of a qualified psychotherapist (psychologist, social worker, marriage, family, child counselor or psychiatrist) is also a very appropriate choice for seeking assistance with anxiety.

As you read this book, take time to reflect upon your situation. Read through it for its concepts and ideas. Then go back and focus on those areas appropriate to you. OVERCOMING ANXIETY includes effective solutions that you can immediately apply in managing and overcoming anxiety. But it is up to you to practice and master the techniques for yourself. Be patient. It took you a lifetime to develop your responses. It will require some time and energy to develop new thinking patterns and behaviors, but the outcome is well worth your effort. You will be more successful in overcoming anxiety and managing your life. Good luck!

Lynn Fossum

Lynn Fossum
Licensed Marriage, Family, Child Counselor
Licensed Educational Psychologist

This book is dedicated to Cheney, Cory and Rick who contributed in their own special way, and to my clients, whose willingness to share their lives has enriched mine and improved my understanding of anxiety.

This book is also dedicated to the memory of the 1989 Loma Prieta earthquake. Through it I (and most residents of the San Francisco Bay area) have a vivid first-hand experience with the subject matter of this book.

CONTENTS

P A R T

I

Understanding Anxiety

UNDERSTANDING ANXIETY

Undoubtedly, you have experienced anxiety. Everyone does. You cannot help but wonder what has happened to you and your nervous system. Why has the very system that is supposed to protect you and keep you safe turned against you? Part of the answer lies in understanding that many of your responses to anxiety are adaptive and designed to help you survive—up to a point. Only in certain circumstances do they become a problem. Very often, magnifying the importance of certain circumstances or events overactivates your system involved in coping with threats and danger. This in turn overrides the normal functioning of these systems and they go bezerk on us. Whammo! Anxiety and panic attack! This book will give you skills and techniques for understanding and overcoming your anxiety.

ANXIETY IS A PARADOX

The amazing thing about anxiety is that usually what you fear the most is the very reaction that occurs when you are having an anxiety attack. In this way anxiety is the ultimate self-fulfilling prophesy. Think about it. For example, what do you fear when you are asked to give a speech? That you will be speechless? That you will forget your speech? That you will be breathless? That your heart will pound and your knees will shake and everyone will know that you are anxious?

When you are having an anxiety attack (or a fear episode) almost every system in your body is affected. These systems include your:

1. **Physiological system** (your body responses), e.g., sweating, increased heart rate, dizziness.

2. **Cognitive system** (your thoughts about the situation), e.g., ''I will make a fool of myself.''

3. **Emotional system** (your feelings), e.g., ''This is terrifying,'' ''I'm so afraid.''

4. **Behavioral system** (your behaviors), e.g., swaying, inhibited speaking, inhibited thinking.

5. **Motivational system** (your prod to action), e.g., ''Get me out of here.''

The sum of these responses is called a **psychobiological reaction.** It is involuntary and it seems to take control of you, and that in itself is very disturbing.

EXERCISE—WHAT HAPPENS TO YOU

Use this checklist to identify your psychobiological reactions to anxiety.
☑ Check your reactions:

Physiological System

☐ Shortness of breath   ☐ Choking

☐ Heart palpitations   ☐ Chest pain

☐ Sweating   ☐ Dizziness

☐ Nausea   ☐ Fainting

☐ Abdominal distress   ☐ Feelings of unreality

☐ Numbness/tingling   ☐ Flushes, hot flashes

☐ Chills   ☐ Other: _____

Cognitive System

☐ *Should/Must Thinking.* Changing decisions or preferences into rigid rules through the use of shoulds and musts. For example: "I have to be on time," "I must finish this report before deadline," "My boss should be polite," "The union should be fair."

☐ *All-Or-Nothing Thinking:* Judging events or people in terms of dichotomous, black-or-white categories. For example, "It's either the *whole* contract, or *nothing* at all." "They have to buy my *entire* package, or no sale." "I've made a *total* fool of myself."

☐ *Overgeneralization:* Deciding that a single negative event is a forever occurrence. For example: "I *never* get acknowledged for my good work," "I *always* get left out of planning projects," "*Every* person in the plant got a raise except me."

☐ *Labeling:* A specific form of overgeneralization, describing yourself with a simplistic, usually negative name. Such labels can include "bossy," "childish," "crazy," "dumb," "failure," "klutz," "nosy," "rotten," "stupid."

☐ *Binocular Thinking:* Magnifying your own flaws and errors while minimizing someone else's, or creating mental catastrophe for yourself while exaggerating someone else's achievement. For example, "I can't stand this, I'll die of embarrassment." "Joe and Harry are truly bright. They get the strategy at once."

☐ *Mind Reading:* A belief that you know what the other people are thinking or feeling without checking it out with them. "I know that Sally thought I was really dumb in today's meeting." "John ignored me today because he's mad at me."

☐ *Fortune Telling:* Anticipating a negative outcome and then acting as if it has already occurred. Confusing the *possible* with the *probable* is the core of fortune telling.

☐ *Using Experts:* Accepting other people's opinions or advice as absolute without checking to see if they are qualified to make such a statement. For example, "Charlie, you know it's not worthwhile to run that equation, it just won't add up. Dump your idea."

☐ *Emotional Reasoning:* Using your feelings as proof that something is true. For example, "I feel really awkward at this conference. That proves I don't belong here. I'm leaving."

☐ *Personalization:* Assuming responsibility for a negative event when there is no basis for your guilt, or confusing *influence* with *control.* "Jerry got so mad when I suggested the new procedure to our boss, I must have said something wrong."

Motivation System

☐ Boredom ☐ Confusion ☐ Dullness
☐ Forgetfulness ☐ Foggy thinking ☐ Lethargy
☐ Weird thoughts ☐ Negative attitude ☐ Poor memory
☐ Reduced concentration ☐ Low productivity

Emotional System

☐ Fear ☐ Anger ☐ Panic
☐ Mood swings ☐ Anxiety ☐ Emptiness
☐ Sadness ☐ Pessimism ☐ Irritability

Behavioral System

☐ Avoiding people ☐ Distrusting others
☐ Increased arguing ☐ Stammering
☐ Inhibited speaking ☐ Swaying
☐ Lashing out ☐ Nagging
☐ Overeating ☐ Drinking
☐ Undereating ☐ Avoiding work
☐ Overworking ☐ Sleeping difficulties

Now that you have identified how you respond to anxiety, you can begin to unlock your chain of reactions.

HOW IT ALL BEGAN

In prehistoric times it was important to fight, flee or faint rapidly in the face of danger. These responses were critical for survival. When circumstances were ambiguous, being startled, which activated psychobiological systems, was better than lying there apathetically to be attacked and eaten.

In today's world, what disturbance is so powerful that it can totally activate your psychobiological systems? The answer is found in your cognitive processes—your *automatic thoughts and images* which occur almost by reflex after your first response. These automatic thoughts and images *seem* to make sense and are followed by a wave of anxiety. By identifying the missing link—the automatic thought or image—that activates your danger response, you can better understand your anxiety and overcome it.

ANXIETY is your total psychobiological response to a situation in which you feel vulnerable to a threat or danger.

THE DIFFERENCE BETWEEN ANXIETY, FEAR, PHOBIA AND PANIC

Very often people lump all reactions into the same category. However, there are some important differences between anxiety, fear, phobia and panic. Understanding the differences in these reactions helps you begin to unlock your understanding of anxiety responses.

Fear comes from the Old English word *faer* which means "sudden calamity or danger." There is a future orientation—dire consequences *might* happen. It is a reference to an actual event or object. It is an appraisal that there is real or potential danger in a certain circumstance or event. ***BECAUSE IT IS AN APPRAISAL, IT IS A COGNITIVE (THOUGHT) PROCESS RATHER THAN AN EMOTIONAL REACTION.***

Anxiety comes from the Latin word *anxius* whose stem word means "to choke" or "to strangle." That choking feeling is what *anxious* refers to—the physiological and feeling responses of agitation and distress. ***ANXIETY IS A PSYCHOBIOLOGICAL REACTION TO AN APPRAISAL OF FEAR.***

Phobia is a reference to a specific fear that is exaggerated and disabling. The Greek word *phobos* means "flight." Phobia is usually characterized by an overwhelming wish to avoid the feared situation.

Panic comes from the name of the Greek god Panikos who was seen by the Greeks as the cause of any sudden, unfounded fear. It has come to mean a "sudden overpowering fright...accompanied by increasing or frantic attempts to secure safety" (*Webster's Third International Dictionary*, 1981).

Test your understanding of the differences. Put the number of the correct definition next to each term:

_____ Fear
1. fear of specific object (dogs, cats, heights), appraisal of high risk in a relatively safe situation

_____ Phobia
2. intense, acute anxiety response; sense of impending catastrophe; overwhelming desire to flee, get help

_____ Anxiety
3. cognitive process; intellectual appraisal of situation

_____ Panic
4. psychobiological response; response to appraisal of fear

Answers: Fear #3, Phobia #1, Anxiety #4, Panic #2

WHAT ANXIETY ISN'T

For many years it was believed that anxiety represented an emotion that had burst out of control. The emphasis had been on understanding the *emotions* of anxiety. Emphasis was placed on understanding feelings and the physiological complaints that went along with them: sweaty palms, trembling hands, heart palpitations, etc.

However, focusing on emotions and physiological complaints drew attention away from the central feature of anxiety: a preoccupation with danger and the responses to it. Researchers found that when a person in the midst of an anxiety attack or response was specifically questioned, the person's awareness was full of threatening thoughts and images. These threatening thoughts and images were frightening, and these frightening thoughts activated the rest of the psychobiological response systems.

A former U.S. President, Franklin D. Roosevelt, was right. "The only thing we have to fear is fear itself." In other words, it's the thoughts and images about danger that activate the anxiety response, *not* the emotions or physiobiological complaints. Thus *if we manage the thoughts and images, we can overcome anxiety.* We cannot manage emotions. We can manage thoughts and images.

WHAT ANXIETY IS

You are made up of systems and subsystems, which fit together to allow you to function and survive. The more effectively your systems are coordinated, the more effectively you function.

Basically there are four main subsystems coordinated by your master system. These are:

- Cognitive (thoughts)

- Affective (feelings)

- Behavioral (actions)

- Physiological (muscle, skeleton)

The subsystems respond according to the demands of a particular time and circumstance. Usually the cognitive system takes the input data first, selects an appropriate response plan and activates the rest of the systems. Your master system usually controls putting together, or integrating, all the responses.

WHAT HAPPENS IN THREAT OR DANGER?

When a threat occurs, you respond with any (and sometimes all) of three major types of reaction:

- Mobilization—preparing you for active defense

- Inhibition—curtailing risky behavior, buying time

- Demobilization—deactivating the motor system, becoming helpless

LET'S SEE HOW IT WORKS

Underlying all anxiety is the potential of threat, or danger either to your physical or psychological well-being. Let's take the example of being caught in a traffic jam.

1. The *Cognitive Subsystem* appraises the situation, checks out the environment, checks the coping resources, determines if there is clear and present danger and activates the affective, behavioral and physiological subsystems. It determines that *if you don't get out of this traffic jam, you will be late to the meeting, lose the account, fall short on your quota, get fired from your job, lose your house, have your family leave you and ruin your life!*

2. The *Affective Subsystem* activates the anxiety component. This speeds up your reactions by enhancing your sense of urgency. You worry that *if you don't get out of this traffic jam FAST, you will be late to the meeting, lose the account, fall short on your quota, get fired from your job, lose your house, have your family leave you and ruin your life! Your just HAVE TO get out of this traffic jam NOW!!!*

3. The *Behavioral Subsystem* activates both action and inhibition patterns. You worry that *if you don't get out of this traffic jam fast, you will be late to the meeting, lose the account, fall short on your quota, get fired from your job, lose your house, have your family leave you and ruin your life! You just have to get out of this traffic jam, SO SWITCH LANES—STEP ON THE ACCELERATOR, NO THE BRAKE, NO THE ACCELERATOR now!!!*

4. The *Physiological Subsystem* mobilizes the body's response mechanisms. You worry that *if you don't get out of this traffic jam fast, you will be late to the meeting, lose the account, fall short on your quota, get fired from your job, lose your house, have your family leave you and ruin your life! You just have to get out of this traffic jam, so switch lanes—step on the accelerator, no the brake, no the accelerator now!!! YOUR HEART IS POUNDING, YOUR HEAD THROBBING, YOUR ADRENELIN PUMPING, YOUR MOUTH IS DRY, MUSCLES TIGHT.* You are really anxious!!! All subsystems are at full tilt anxiety mode.

One of the problems with anxiety is that the switch from one subsystem to another gets jumbled. For example, the physiological system stays mobilized (tense, pulse increased, stomach churning) long after the cognitive system has signaled that the danger has passed. In other words, the feedback loop is disconnected. Sometimes, several conflicting response modes are activated simultaneously. When speaking in public you may experience both a desire to protect yourself from ridicule and a conflicting response to show your intelligence by responding to a question. As long as you feel vulnerable to a "clear and present danger" you may be unable to overrride or inactivate your behavioral subsystem—so you become speechless or stammer.

In anxiety, your subsystems malfunction in the way they begin or end a defense to a threat. The symptoms of anxiety are expressions either of an excessive functioning of your subsystems (too much of a good thing) or interference with the functioning of your subsystems.

EXERCISE AHEAD

EXERCISE—YOUR SUBSYSTEM RESPONSE

Use this checklist to see how your four subsystems malfunction in response to threat or danger. Check ☑ any you have experienced.

Cognitive System Malfunctions

1. Sensory-Perceptual
    - ☐ In a daze, haze, fog, cloud
    - ☐ Self-consciousness
    - ☐ On guard
    - ☐ Feeling of unreality
    - ☐ Objects seem distant or blurred
    - ☐ Other _____

2. Thinking difficulties
    - ☐ Difficulty concentrating
    - ☐ Confused
    - ☐ Can't recall names, important ideas
    - ☐ Mind races, uncontrolled thoughts
    - ☐ Difficulty reasoning
    - ☐ Lose objectivity and perspective
    - ☐ Easily distracted
    - ☐ Blocking ideas

3. Conceptual
    - ☐ Distortion of thoughts
    - ☐ Frightening visual images (not hallucinations)
    - ☐ Repetition of fearful concepts
    - ☐ Fear of losing control

    Going crazy   Injury
    Being unable to cope   Negative evaluation
    Death

Affective System Malfunctions

- ☐ Alarmed
- ☐ Edgy
- ☐ Frightened
- ☐ Jittery
- ☐ Nervous
- ☐ Tense
- ☐ Uneasy
- ☐ Anxious
- ☐ Fearful
- ☐ Impatient
- ☐ Jumpy
- ☐ Scared
- ☐ Terrified
- ☐ Wound up

Behavioral System Malfunctions

- ☐ Avoidance
- ☐ Hyperventilation
- ☐ Inhibition
- ☐ Restlessness
- ☐ Immobility
- ☐ Flight
- ☐ Impaired coordination
- ☐ Postural collapse
- ☐ Speech dysfluency

Physiological System Malfunctions

1. Cardiovascular
   - ☐ Decreased/increased blood pressure
   - ☐ Decreased pulse rate
   - ☐ Racing heart
   - ☐ Faintness/fainting
   - ☐ Palpitations

2. Respiratory
   - ☐ Choking sensation
   - ☐ Rapid breathing
   - ☐ Difficulty in getting air in
   - ☐ Shallow breathing
   - ☐ Gasping
   - ☐ Shortness of breath
   - ☐ Lump in throat
   - ☐ Bronchial spasms
   - ☐ Pressure on chest

3. Neuromuscular
   - ☐ Clumsy motions
   - ☐ Eyelid twitching
   - ☐ Fidgeting
   - ☐ Generalized weakness
   - ☐ Increased reflexes
   - ☐ Insomnia
   - ☐ Pacing
   - ☐ Rigidity
   - ☐ Spasm
   - ☐ Startle reaction
   - ☐ Strained face
   - ☐ Tremors
   - ☐ Unsteady
   - ☐ Wobbly legs

4. Gastrointestinal
   - ☐ Abdominal discomfort
   - ☐ Abdominal pain
   - ☐ Heartburn
   - ☐ Loss of appetite
   - ☐ Revulsion toward food
   - ☐ Nausea
   - ☐ Vomiting

5. Urinary tract
   - ☐ Pressure to urinate
   - ☐ Frequent urination

6. Skin
   - ☐ Flushed face
   - ☐ Hot and cold spells
   - ☐ Pale face
   - ☐ Itching
   - ☐ Generalized sweating
   - ☐ Sweaty palms

If you are like most people, you have probably checked almost every item. Do not think you are abnormal, crazy or weird. All people experience anxiety. Our subsystems all kick in similarly to protect us from threats. But why?

14

WHAT ANXIETY DOES FOR US

At their root, many of today's anxiety responses ensure basic survival—survival of the species even at the expense of the individual. Many fear reactions keep in check overly careless or expansive patterns. We are equipped with automatic regulators that keep us from advancing too far. For example, the ''visual cliff reflex'' (an automatic regulator) was experimentally proven by Marks in 1969. He found that infant mammals, including humans, become immobile when they come to the edge of a ledge. This inhibits them from advancing into a danger zone before they are mature enough to understand the danger. As the mammal matures, this regulator usually disappears when the ability to evaluate the situation develops. However, when this primitive, or early, regulator continues into adulthood, it is displayed as dizziness and overly cautious or inhibited movement near the edge of a cliff, which is an anxiety response.

Many other childhood fears serve the same protective purpose. Think of common childhood fears. How many did you experience as a child? How many do you still experience?

- ☐ Falling
- ☐ Being injured
- ☐ Drowning
- ☐ Suffocating
- ☐ Darkness
- ☐ Deep water
- ☐ Strangers
- ☐ Separating from caretakers

- ☐ Getting lost
- ☐ Abandonment
- ☐ Negative evaluation
- ☐ Other _____

_____

_____

_____

_____

These fears reveal internal and external threats, personal and interpersonal danger. They go in both directions—discouraging hazardous, risky behavior and discouraging foolish, childish behavior.

In 1929 W.B. Cannon formulated the concept of ''fight or flee'' as a response to danger. He observed that animals were equipped either to fight threats from other animals or flee. Either way they activated a similar set of physiological response mechanisms (increased heart rate, tensed muscles, etc.).

There is, additionally, another set of protective mechanisms designed to cope with danger. These are the automatic reactions that protect against the entering of harmful substances (eyeblink), the ejecting of harmful substances (gagging, coughing, bronchospasm, vomiting, diarrhea), defending against external blows (ducking, dodging, flinching, retracting, stiffening), inhibiting movement (fainting), and reaching to others for help (grabbing).

Thus we really have a set of automatic responses that can more appropriately be called ''fight—flee—freeze—fling—faint,'' **the five F's.** These reactions are very primitive and quite unlearned. As we grow older they can become more complex and more intentional than reflexive. An example of this is when you realize you are not in complete control of your car and you reduce your speed to regain a sense of control. Or when you feel dizzy at the top of a tall ladder and you take a better grip.

Anxiety is an attention getter. It functions very similarly to physical pain. Sometimes we get confused and think the problem is anxiety. This is like thinking the pain is the disease. Remember, the role of pain is to call your attention to a problem, to allow you to repair the injury, fight off the infection. Likewise, anxiety is designed to help you reduce the danger. However, *when the problem is not the actual danger but your distortion or exaggeration of it, then you have no way to cope with it effectively.* The anxiety no longer serves to protect you from threat. In fact, it gets in your way of accurately assessing the danger and selecting an appropriate response.

HOW ANXIETY GETS
IN THE WAY

Whenever there is danger, it is a normal reaction to feel fear. Not only is it normal, it is adaptive. It signals trouble, prepares you to respond and helps you survive. Usually when the danger subsides or disappears, so does the anxiety.

Anxiety becomes a problem when you persistently perceive situations as threatening when they are not. It is also a problem when your anxiety remains after the danger has passed. Anxiety can then interfere with your effective functioning. In a vicious downward spiral anxiety interferes with your ability to respond appropriately to the next actual danger or threat.

When all your attention is focused, however involuntarily, on the *concepts of danger or threat*, it becomes very difficult for you to focus on your work, enjoy yourself or reflect upon your situation. It is as though you are in possession of a super-sensitive alarm system. It goes off at the slightest movement or intrusion. It cannot distinguish between the family dog or an armed robber—and neither can you! So you stay on constant alert and your automatic thoughts about danger are constantly activated. Usually they are activated so quickly and frequently that you are not aware of them. Psychologists call this state **hypervigilance.**

Illogical **automatic thoughts** are another interference that comes with anxiety. In addition to having frequent ''false alarms,'' your ability to ''reason'' with your thoughts is impaired. You may recognize that your fearful thoughts are illogical, but you may not be able to evaluate them very well without help. The automatic thoughts continue involuntarily and keep the pressure on. It is the involuntary nature of these thoughts that lead so many anxious people to think they are ''losing their mind.''

Another way anxiety responses get in the way is that they **generalize** to other things. Hearing a siren suggests to you that your house might be on fire. An airplane overhead reminds you that you might crash on your next business trip. If you have experienced a traumatic or frightening event, memory of it or visual images (daydreams) about it may evoke anxiety as intense as during the original event. This is the kind of anxiety called ''Post-traumatic Stress Disorder'' experienced by many Vietnam veterans and survivors from similar traumatic experiences.

Several other confusions in thinking are characteristic of anxiety:

Catastrophizing or concentrating on the worst possible outcome is a frequent occurrence. As you are about to make an important business presentation, you become afraid of making a fool out of yourself, forgetting what you have to say, fainting or running screaming from the room, thus ruining your entire career and your entire life.

Loss of perspective is also common. You respond to all the potential dangers and threats in situations but overlook the potential benefits and advantages of circumstances. You remember all the mistakes you made in talking with your boss about the new project but overlook all her encouragement of your ideas and efforts.

When you lose your tolerance for uncertainty or ambiguity and begin to indulge in **all-or-nothing** thinking, little intrusions become major threats. The rustling of files in the outer office signals someone taking top secret documents, shortness of breath at the business meeting means you may stop breathing entirely. Hence all dangers tend to be seen in absolute, extreme terms.

The final difficulty with faulty thinking is called **lack of habituation.** Researchers have found that with repeated exposure to moderately frightening situations, nonanxious people tend to habituate, or adapt. Highly anxious people, on the other hand, become more anxious. It seems that nonanxious people are able to determine rather rapidly that the circumstance does not necessarily pose a threat. Anxious persons, on the other hand, are not able to distinguish between when a circumstance is or is not safe.

P A R T

II

Overcoming Anxiety

OVERCOMING ANXIETY

The following story illustrates how important the context, or circumstances, are in determining anxiety.

A hunter was out in the wild, hunting lions. Suddenly, from out of the dark shadows, a lion pounced. The hunter's heart was pounding and his hands were trembling as he raised his tranquilizer dart gun. He found himself uncertain of his aim, doubting his abilities and was sure he was about to be shredded by the lion's sharp claws. Just as it lunged for him, the lion dropped to the ground and fell into a stupor, felled by the dart gun fired by the hunter's trusty guide and companion. She had witnessed the terrifying scene from the safari truck, quickly grabbed her gun, took aim and felled the lion just in the nick of time. Later, back at the zoo, the lion hunter stood outside the lion compound, admiring his prize catch as it paced within the confines of the well-appointed cage surrounded by a wide, deep moat and an eight-foot fence.

What do you think accounts for the difference in the hunter's anxiety level when observing the lion in the wild and at the zoo?

Of course. It is a person's appraisal, or construction, of a potentially dangerous situation. Our appraisal and reappraisal of a situation determines our concept of the danger in it. It is this *cognitive set* or way of seeing the picture that determines our perception of threat or danger. This *cognitive set* is a composite of our expectations, interests and concerns which are put together to give us a picture. This set determines what we will focus on, what we will gloss over and what we will exclude. Each time we are in a circumstance we bring to it a *cognitive set* that has been built from our experiences over time. Our initial impressions provide information that either supports or changes a pre-existing cognitive set. This first impression is important because, unless modified or reversed, it sets up the series of thinking steps that leads us to perceive a circumstance and respond to it with or without anxiety. Remember this concept of *cognitive set*.

Understanding your cognitive set is critical in overcoming anxiety.

COGNITIVE SET—AT WORK IN STRESS AND ANXIETY

When you perceive (correctly or incorrectly) that there is danger, you will immediately set up an "emergency response." This danger can be anything that threatens your survival, individuality, functioning or interpersonal attachments (loves and friendships). What is essential about this emergency response is that it is self-centered; that is, it is designed for your survival. You must respond immediately and without thought so there is no room for interruption, contemplation or wishywashiness.

This oversimplified thinking activates a less mature but more rapidly responding system response than does a stressful or neutral situation. This primitive response is the anxiety response, and it is the global, absolute and arbitrary nature of it that makes it different from the stress response.

With stress you have time to think and contemplate your response. With anxiety you activate primitive systems. Later on as you reappraise the situation, the false alarms may be turned off.

However, with anxiety problems, the contradictory information does not compute. Somehow, the data that is inconsistent with the *cognitive set* is not taken in and used. At this point it becomes important to stop and ask yourself some serious questions:

1. **Does this situation pose an immediate threat to my vital interests?**

2. **Could I possibly sustain physical harm?**

3. **Could I possibly sustain psychological harm—for example, rejection, devaluation?**

4. **Does it violate rules that protect my vital interests?**

BREAKING THE BEHAVIOR/EMOTIONS CYCLE

At the same time that you are figuring out how great the threat is you are also figuring out how well you can meet it. What are your resources? Have you overcome this before? Have you failed before? This whole process is rapid and automatic. Your final decision about your risk, and therefore your anxiety, is determined by your appraisal of both the danger (and probability of it happening) and your ability to cope with it.

If you determine that the danger is low compared to your coping mechanisms, you will probably choose to eliminate the danger by attacking the source, i.e., "fight," using hostile responses. On the other hand, if you determine the danger to be great compared to your ability to cope with it, most likely you will reduce the degree of danger by escape ("flight"), self-inhibition ("freeze") or collapse ("faint")—more generally fear responses.

An interesting thing occurs with the decision to fight. Usually the decision to fight occurs when you feel you can overcome the danger, be it a hostile takeover or an angry co-worker. Your self-confidence in your abilities plays a key role in your decision. Your fighting serves to reduce your anger. However, sometimes a fight response also occurs when you feel trapped. If you feel you can't flee, freeze or faint, you may fight as a last resort, hoping to slow down or deter the danger. *In this case you aren't feeling anger, you are feeling anxious. Your fighting is a way to reduce your anxiety.*

THE DIFFERENCE BETWEEN BEHAVIOR AND EMOTIONS

Have you ever been in a stage play or gone to a particularly dramatic movie? You saw the actors expressing emotions. But you did not see the actors' emotions. We can never see the emotions of the other person, only the behavior they use to express their emotions. Thus we see that behavior and emotions are two separate systems. One may reflect the other, although not always. But one is not the same as the other. An emotion has a physiological response that you cannot control (try to keep your hands from sweating), but you may *choose* the behavior or actions you use to express the emotion you are feeling.

Popular thinking has it that emotions are like a fluid reservoir. When enough pressure builds up in the reservoir then the emotions become expressed outwardly. Similarly, failure to express these emotions pushes them to be expressed in other ways through bodily ailments. However, while free and open expression of anger may be helpful in reducing some psychosomatic disorders like headache, ulcers and colitis, it has *not* been shown that free and open expression of anxiety has the same relieving effect.

Anxiety creates a vicious cycle. As your physiological responses begin (heart pounding, sweating, etc.) your cognitive processes (thinking) mobilize your behavior. But the more aware you become of being anxious, the more physiological anxiety responses occur, and the more aware you become of being anxious. And on the cycle goes.

How many times have you seemed anxious such as fearing you will have a squeaky voice when giving a speech. As you started to give the speech, you realized your voice was squeaky. It was squeaky because you were anxious. Then you became more anxious about what you were anxious about in the first place—the squeaky voice, which has now become REALLY squeaky! The more your attention is given to your anxiety, the more your outward show of anxiety will be.

THE EMERGENCY-RESPONSE SYSTEM & THE ANXIETY-RESPONSE SYSTEM

When you perceive yourself to be threatened or in danger, your Emergency-Response System begins responding immediately. These responses—"the five F's," referred to on page 15—are so necessary for survival that they occur rapidly and automatically. Activations of the sympathetic or parasympathetic branches of our nervous system, they either prepare us to cope with the danger (fight/flight) or assist us when active coping won't work (blink) or would be counterproductive (faint).

Your Emergency-Response System includes:

Fight—if trapped, a protective action to ward off the blow, deter further attack or defend yourself.

Flight—the most common response to danger when feasible. It includes emotionally fleeing through withdrawal or silence.

Freeze—usually occurs before an attack, giving time to appraise the situation or prepare for its impact. Occurs automatically and inhibits movement, speech or memory. Serves as a protection against hazards such as walking off a cliff.

Faint—when feeling helpless, overwhelmed or, for some, when exposed to mutilation or blood.

Retraction—drawing back from dangers like heights, attacking dog.

Ducking, dodging, jumping—to evade projectiles or falling things.

Clutching, clinging—grasping to maintain balance, prevent falling, drowning, etc.

Reflexes—including eyeblink, gagging, coughing.

Distress calls—spontaneous calls for help.

ANXIETY-RESPONSE SYSTEM

The Emergency-Response System and the Anxiety-Response System are triggered at the same time. The Emergency-Response System is an immediate primitive response system that buys you time while the slower acting Anxiety-Response System is forming an appropriate adaptive strategy.

The Anxiety-Response System operates by:

1. Creating a feeling

2. Forcing your attention to the danger

3. Strategizing to reduce the danger

Feeling ⟶ Attention to danger ⟶ Strategy to reduce danger

It is important to understand that when anxiety is aroused its role is to prod you into taking action to reduce the danger. However, anxiety itself is not a part of the action plan. In other words, feeling anxious does not make the danger go away. Rather, you continue to feel anxious until you perceive (your cognitive set tells you) that you are no longer in danger. This "all clear" signal occurs when either the danger disappears (you are given a bonus rather than the boot you were anxious about) or your cognitive set shifts to perceive no danger (you recognize yourself to be a valuable employee). *Your cognitive set (thinking) is the key to your anxiety management.*

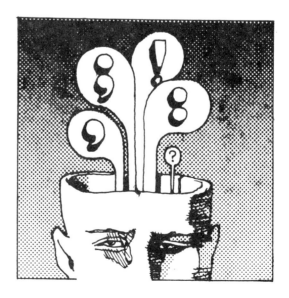

CLEARING YOUR MIND

It should now be apparent that a large part of a persisting sense of anxiety is created by your perceptions about your situation, i.e., your cognitive set. This set is determined by your past life experiences, your responses, the consequences, your feelings about them and the feedback about them that you allow.

The optimist's half-full cup as compared to the pessimist's half-empty cup is one way of conceptualizing the idea of cognitive set. We tend to apply our cognitive set to a variety of experiences, and this set contributes to our perception of circumstances as dangerous or benign.

Many of the rules we have developed that contribute to our particular cognitive set were originally developed through visual images, sensations or sounds. Later on, we may have formulated them in words, but rules do not always take a verbal form. For example, you may find yourself quite anxious around airports. Careful reflection may reveal that the loud roaring sound of airplane engines was a sound that, with no comprehension of the idea of airports, you found extremely terrifying as an infant.

Once we develop a cognitive set, we create *assumptions* that support it. The optimist assumes that the half-full cup contains plenty to go around. The pessimist assumes that the half-empty cup will run out before he gets a drink.

These assumptions become *operating assumptions*. They set the tone for how we act by creating *self instructions*. These assumptions and rules fall into three categories:

1. General Warnings—e.g., co-workers can be dangerous.

2. Specific Warnings—e.g., if I interrupt they'll hurt me.

3. Inhibiting Injunctions—e.g., shut up.

You will find that gaining some understanding of how your cognitive set contributes to your anxiety will help you overcome that anxiety.

EXERCISE—CLEARING YOUR MIND

Specify a situation in which you feel anxious, e.g., speaking to co-workers: _____

_____

✔✔Now follow this *Four-Step Process:*

1. Identify your *Operating Assumption:* (e.g., People do not like to have their privacy invaded.) _____

_____

_____

_____

2. Determine the *Special Case Application:* (e.g., If I interrupt my co-workers' conversation to ask for help, they could get angry and retaliate. They could harm me in my career, so it is safer to overestimate their power than underestimate it.) _____

_____

_____

_____

3. Identify your *Conclusion:* (e.g., I'd better not interrupt.) _____

_____

_____

_____

4. Identify your *Self-Instruction:* (e.g., Shut up!—Resulting in inhibition.) _____

_____

_____

_____

Often this self-instruction leads to more rules that feed into your cognitive set (don't bother people, keep your mouth shut) that lead to more inhibitions. *Any time you find yourself trying to overcome your self-instruction, you feel you are breaking your cognitive-set rules and you feel more anxious.* **Stay with the anxiety, it will pass and you will be OK.**

VULNERABILITY—UNDERNEATH IT ALL

In all anxiety the rules are about danger and vulnerability, your estimate of your capacity to cope with the danger and compensate for your vulnerability. The rules are generally conditional, ''if something happens, it may hurt me.'' If when it happens it doesn't hurt you, you can still hold onto the rule because of the *MAY*. After all, who knows about next time.

Because you feel so threatened and so vulnerable, you operate at a very primitive level. The rules you invoke are very basic, broad, overgeneralized and quite inflexible. Your more mature ideas are displaced. The more vulnerable you feel, the more you accept the validity of your primitive rules.

What is vulnerability? It is a perception of yourself as subject to dangers, internal or external, over which you have no or so little control that you have no sense of safety.

When you feel vulnerable, you can count on several responses:

- Your thinking becomes clouded

- You lose perspective

- It is difficult to be objective about yourself and the situation

- Your self-confidence dwindles

VULNERABILITY (Continued)

Several factors contribute to your sense of vulnerability: skill sets, self-doubt, context and experience. Let's explore these factors further.

1. **Skill Sets**—If you believe that you lack important skills to cope with a particular threat, then your sense of vulnerability is greatly increased. For example, if your boss offers you the opportunity to take the project proposal to the team in Japan, but you lack skills in the Japanese language, your anxiety about the success of your presentation is going to increase. Likewise, if your work unit is putting together a softball team and you feel very inadequate at softball, your vulnerability about being accepted as part of the team will contribute to your anxiety.

2. **Self-Doubt**—Your ability to react with self-confidence instead of vulnerability depends on how you assess your ability to cope with the threatening or dangerous situation. Here's how the sequence goes: 1. You approach the dangerous situation. 2. You assess the degree of danger and your resources to cope adequately with it. 3. You perceive the danger is greater than your skills to cope with it. This triggers your vulnerability mode. 4. Once this mode is on, you process all incoming data in terms of your weaknesses rather than your strengths. You shift to self-doubt. You hold back your ideas in the next business meeting. You don't challenge your colleagues. You negate your contributions.

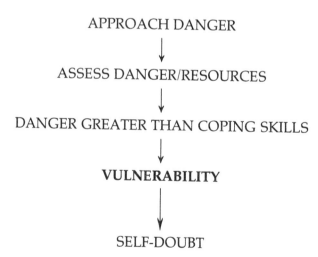

APPROACH DANGER

↓

ASSESS DANGER/RESOURCES

↓

DANGER GREATER THAN COPING SKILLS

↓

VULNERABILITY

↓

SELF-DOUBT

3. **Context and Experience**—Self-doubt sabotages your belief in yourself and your competency. The possible exposure to criticism and humiliation by others may totally interfere with your speaking in class or business meetings, although you may be fine in the company of your family. When you first began using the new computer program, you held back and worked far more tentatively compared to your current performance after six months' experience with it.

MAINTAINING CONFIDENCE IS CRUCIAL

If this is so, how can you maintain confidence rather than give in to the vulnerability set? Your ability to retain confidence is related to several factors:

☐ 1. You are strong enough in your belief in your own competencies to mitigate against vulnerability. Remember Jonathan Livingston Seagull flies because he thinks he can.

☐ 2. You keep the context as nonevaluative rather than evaluative by others. Your performance is not being negatively judged by others.

☐ 3. You keep your focus on being problem-oriented rather than danger-oriented. This is a problem to be solved, not a threat to your life or well-being.

> You maintain your self-confidence by focusing on the positives, minimizing the dangers and assuming you have control of the situation.

PSYCHOLOGICAL VULNERABILITY

It should now be apparent that your performance is not only impaired by a perception of a lack of skills or competency. It is equally impaired by *active interference* with the skills you do have. Even though you may be well skilled, your *anticipation* that you might do poorly and get hurt is enough to block your performance. When you begin to question your ability to perform adequately or safely you begin to experience inhibitions and anxiety. Your warning flags go up and signal you to stop moving into the danger zone. Your anxiety is unpleasant and signals you to stop. When you stop or retreat, your anxiety goes down. When you go forward, your anxiety increases. *If you make a conscious decision to go on, you may be able to override your primitive inhibition reactions.*

Your automatic actions are very connected to your thoughts. If your attitude is "all's well," you go forward without any internal inhibitions. But if you think you might have danger you can't overcome, you are automatically inhibited. This is true whether the danger is physical at the edge of a cliff or social at the beginning of a speech.

The more you predict disaster, the more you inhibit and the more disastrous the situation seems, so the more you inhibit, and on and on in a vicious cycle. While this inhibition may have initially served to protect you, it has now gotten in your way.

PUBLIC/PRIVATE WORLDS— SOCIAL/INDIVIDUAL SELF

For those of us with physical dangers at work, we make conscious choices and take precautionary measures to enable us to reduce the risk of harm. However, most of us are working in areas where the interpersonal or social dangers present the greatest threat. Therefore, let's take a look at those areas of vulnerability and our responses to them.

We all live in both a public and a private world. Our *private world* includes those people in our family and our close friends. Our *public world* includes our colleagues at work, church, clubs and organizations. Within these two worlds we attempt for a balance between our social self and individual self. Our *social self* depends on interactions with other people for satisfying goals and strivings, solving problems and survival. It also needs others for intimacy, sharing understanding, approval, affection and the like. Our *individual self* advances our own sense of identity, mastery and independence. It defines and protects its domain, establishes its status, rights and privileges, masters the body and skills and acquires power and control over the environment.

In both the public and private world we have threats to our social and individual self. Since these threats create the underpinnings of our sense of vulnerability and the resultant anxiety, let's look at what the threats include.

Our *social self* can be threatened in the public world by the possible loss of things that are socially gratifying. These include no longer being part of a group, not being accepted by the group, losing the group conviviality. The worst possible threat is exclusion and isolation.

In the private world our social self can be threatened by loss or negative interactions with important personal people. The worst possible threats are deprivation, disapproval, rejection and desertion.

Our *individual self* can likewise be threatened in the public world. Threats to our identity, success, recognition, achievement all represent dangers. The worst possible threat is shame, in which pride is injured by defeat, loss of status or thwarting of ambition. You feel devalued by depreciation, defeat, or domination.

Our individual self is also at risk in the private world. The possibility of disability, dysfunction, disease or death are the worst possible threats. They are triggered by loss of control and loss of self-mastery.

YOUR ANXIETY PRONE AREAS

Use the following matrix to identify the areas in which you are anxiety prone:

Give examples of possible threats to your social and individual self. Write how these threats might be shown:

	Social Self	**Individual** Self
Identify areas of **Public** Vulnerability: _____ _____	Disapproval _____ _____	Default _____ _____
	Exclusion _____ _____	Defeat _____ _____
	Isolation _____ _____	Depreciation _____ _____
	Separation _____ _____	Thwarting _____ _____
	Deprivation _____ _____	Death _____ _____
Identify areas of **Private** Vulnerability: _____ _____	Desertion _____ _____	Disability _____ _____
	Disapproval _____ _____	Disease _____ _____
	Rejection _____ _____	Dysfunction _____ _____

In the next chapter, you will learn specific techniques to help you clear your mind and overcome anxiety.

CLEARING YOUR BODY

As you recall, an anxiety attack involves all of your psychobiologic systems:

- Physiological
- Cognitive
- Motivational
- Emotional
- Behavioral

In the previous section we discussed ways of clearing your mind. These strategies address contributions of the cognitive, motivational and emotional subsystems to your anxiety.

Now we will discuss contributions of the physiological and behavioral subsystems to your anxiety. Let's review those on the psychobiologic checklist of reactions:

Behavioral System

- ☐ Avoiding people
- ☐ Increased arguing
- ☐ Inhibited speaking
- ☐ Lashing out
- ☐ Eating
- ☐ Distrusting others
- ☐ Stammering
- ☐ Swaying
- ☐ Nagging
- ☐ Drinking

Physiological System

- ☐ Shortness of breath
- ☐ Heart palpitations
- ☐ Sweating
- ☐ Nausea
- ☐ Abdominal Distress
- ☐ Numbness/tingling
- ☐ Chills
- ☐ Choking
- ☐ Chest pain
- ☐ Dizziness
- ☐ Fainting
- ☐ Feelings of unreality
- ☐ Flushes, hot flashes
- ☐ Other _____

These reactions were originally designed to assist you in danger. They were part of the Emergency-Response System, the primitive system designed to immediately respond.

You have learned how by activating your Emergency-Response System you also simultaneously activate your Anxiety-Response System. If your cognitive subsystem does not signal "all clear" then your Anxiety-Response System goes into full swing.

Your cognitive subsystem can have great difficulty reading your physiological subsystem signals. Very frequently those responses are misread as *proof* of the danger rather than immediate responses to *possible* danger.

HYPERVENTILATION

The most frequent miscuing occurs to a response called **hyperventilation**. What is hyperventilation? Quite simply it is too much (hyper) ventilation (air movement).

If you breathe more rapidly or more deeply you may begin to hyperventilate if you do not also increase your physical activity at the same time. These breathing responses are necessary at times in response to danger (remember fight or flee). However, with prolonged anxiety, they fail to serve their original purpose.

Several physiological reactions occur during hyperventilation. The first is a dramatic change in the carbon dioxide level in your bloodstream. It can drop as much as 50% in 30 seconds with forceful hyperventilation. Carbon dioxide is used by the body to regulate your breathing. So a dramatic shift signals a change in your breathing regulation.

More significantly, carbon dioxide is important in maintaining the acid/base, or pH, level in your blood. When this pH level in the nerve cells is increased by hyperventilation, the nerve cells become more excitable. This triggers the fight or flight response and the chain reaction begins:

- Heart palpitations, racing heart
- Heartburn, chest pain
- Numbness, tingling in mouth, hands or feet
- Sweating
- Dizziness, faintness, lightheadedness
- Poor concentration, blurred vision, feelings of unreality
- Shortness of breath
- Difficulty swallowing, lump in the throat
- Stomach pain, nausea
- Fatigue, poor sleep, nightmares
- Tense muscles, muscle spasms, shaking

Too often these hyperventilation responses are miscued as the danger rather than a response to it. Your Anxiety-Response System now begins to operate.

To test whether hyperventilation is a contributor to your anxiety symptoms, do the following:

1. Check your normal breathing pattern:
   a. Put one hand on your chest and the other hand on your stomach.
   b. Breathe slightly deeper than normal.
   c. Which hand moves the most?
      - ☐ Stomach—you are using your diaphragm. Usually hyperventilation is not a contributor to anxiety symptoms.
      - ☐ Chest—You are an upper chest breather. Probably hyperventilation contributes to your symptoms.
      - ✔ Learn to breathe diaphragmatically. See page 38.

2. Count your breathing rate. (8-16 breaths/minute is normal.)
   - ☐ Average resting breathing rate higher than 28 breaths/minute suggests difficulties from hyperventilation.
   - ✔ Practice slowing your breating rate to 8-16 breaths/minute. See page 40.

3. Deliberately hyperventilate.*
   a. Breathe 60 times/minute for three minutes—one breath per second. (Stop at any time if you feel very anxious.)
   b. Notice your sensations. Almost everyone notices dry mouth and throat, some lightheadedness.
      - ☐ If you also experience sensations you associate with anxiety, hyperventilation probably contributes to your anxiety symptoms.
      - ✔ Learn Relaxed Diaphragmatic Breathing. See page 38.

To overcome your tendency to hyperventilate through shallow upper chest breathing or rapid breathing, learn Relaxed Diaphragmatic Breathing. To change your way of breathing, this exercise should be practiced regularly.

---

*Breathing into a paper bag restores your carbon dioxide balance. Keep a paper bag handy if you wish to stop the symptoms.

While this test is perfectly safe for most people, some medical conditions such as angina (heart pain) and epilepsy (seizures) can worsen with hyperventilation. If you have any doubts about your safety, consult your physician before doing this test.

✔✔ Relaxed Diaphragmatic Breathing

The goal of the following exercise is to help you:

- Know when you are breathing with your diaphragm without placing your hand on your abdomen.
- Recognize a Relaxed Diaphragmatic Breath.
- Use Relaxed Diaphragmatic Breathing effortlessly whenever you choose.

Do this exercise twice a day. Wear loose, comfortable clothes and lie down. (In bed, just before arising and just before going to sleep are good times.)

Spend about one minute on each practice session. Do not breathe too deeply or too rapidly (i.e., avoid hyperventilating). Take four or five comfortable Relaxed Diaphragmatic Breaths. Do not make an ordeal of this.

1. Lie down.
2. Place one hand over your abdomen at your belly button.
3. Breathe so that your hand moves up and down in a relaxed manner.
   a. If you find it difficult to move your hand up and down with your abdomen, suck in your abdomen when you breathe out. Relax and notice how your abdomen expands as you breathe in.
   b. If you wonder if your chest is moving too much (it will move slightly) place your other hand on your chest. This hand should move less than the hand on your abdomen.

After you can breathe with your diaphragm while lying down, practice two or three times per day while standing. Practicing just before you sit down to eat breakfast, lunch and dinner is a good way to get in your three practice sessions.

After you can breathe with your diaphragm while standing, practice two or three times per day while sitting. For some upper-chest breathers, this can be the most difficult position. Keep practicing until it is easy, even when sitting. Again, practicing when you sit down to eat breakfast, lunch and dinner is a good way to work in your three practice sessions.

When you master this, congratulations! You can now use Relaxed Diaphragmatic Breathing whenever you begin to feel anxious or panicky. Observe the difference it makes in your anxiety.

THE ROLE OF
REST AND RELAXATION

You have become familiar with the role of hyperventilation as a contributor to anxiety responses. Rest and relaxation also play a role. Specifically, lack of rest and difficulty with relaxation contribute to anxiety.

Anxiety places demands upon your body and requires energy—energy that your body must provide by either having an adequate supply or using it for anxiety instead of another purpose. When you ''rob Peter to pay Paul'' you merely contribute to your anxiety. Being adequately rested allows you to have the energy to respond appropriately to potential danger. You can use your cognitive set adequately and not trigger your Anxiety-Response System. Just as you find your resistance to colds and flu is much greater when you are adequately rested, so is your resistance to anxiety. The energy supply is there to overcome your anxiety.

Many people confuse *recreation* and *relaxation*. While recreation is pleasurable and frequently a good escape from stress and pressure, relaxation in the form of a deep relaxation response is vital for overcoming the fight/flight response which triggers anxiety.

There are many methods that can produce deep relaxation responses. These can include:

- Yoga
- Meditation
- Biofeedback
- Self-hypnosis
- Progressive muscle relaxation

DEEP RELAXATION RESPONSES

One of the simplest methods is slow breathing. Its advantage is that it can be used at any time, alone or in groups, without special equipment or calling attention to you. (Deep breathing in meetings sometimes creates huge sighs and produces startled looks from others. And as you just learned, it can cause hyperventilation.)

✔✔Slow Breathing

1. Inhale slowly using Relaxed Diaphragmatic Breathing. Count slowly as you inhale, seeing how long you can maintain your inhalation.
2. At the end of your inhalation, stop a half second.
3. Now exhale, slowly counting quietly to yourself.
4. After exhaling, stop, relax your muscles.
5. Repeat steps one through four three more times.
6. Notice how much calmer and relaxed you feel.

Four More Relaxation Exercises

The next relaxation responses require some practice to master. But they are well worth the effort. They will help you achieve a state of relaxation and calm which help overcome your anxiety and provide energy for other parts of your life.

The four relaxation responses are:

- Progressive Relaxation
- Focus
- Fantasy
- Counting Backward

✔✔Progressive Relaxation

This exercise is based on the finding that a muscle will become more relaxed after it is first tensed. Do not expect to master this exercise at first. It takes practice but is well worth it.

1. Pick a time and place in which you will not be disturbed.

2. Lie or sit in a comfortable position.

3. Close your eyes and use Relaxed Diaphragmatic Breathing.

4. Tune in to your body. Notice which muscles are most tense.

5. You will tighten, hold, then relax one muscle group at a time.
   Complete a breathing cycle before moving to the next muscle group.
   Begin with your toes. Tighten, hold, then relax. Now breathe.
   Now do your ankles. Tighten, hold, then relax. Now breathe.
   Next your calves.
   Now your thighs.
   Next your buttocks.
   Your abdomen.
   Your stomach. Remember to tighten, hold, then relax. Now breathe.
   Next your chest.
   Now your lower back.
   Your upper back.
   Shoulders.
   Next your upper arms.
   Your lower arms.
   Your wrists.
   Now clench your fists, hold, relax. Now breathe.
   Do your neck.
   Now scrunch up your face, hold, relax, breathe.

Now breathe two more cycles. Notice how much more relaxed you were than when you began. If any muscles still feel tense, tighten them, hold, relax and breathe. Are you feeling more relaxed now?

✔✔Focus

This is a technique used in many types of religious or secular meditation practiced throughout the world.

1. Pick a time and place in which you will not be disturbed.

2. Lie or sit in a comfortable position.

3. Close your eyes and with each breath you exhale, repeat a word or phrase that keeps your mind focused in your internal center. You will shift your mind from external, logical thought or mind-wandering. You may repeat words such as "calm," "relax," "peace" or phrases that have a religious or spiritual meaning for you. Or you may repeat syllables such as "ohm."

4. If you prefer to keep your eyes open, focus on a specific object or place in the room such as a picture, the ceiling, a chair. Let your eyes soften and haze the image.

5. Do not worry if you lose your concentration. This happens. Just redirect your focus to your breathing and your word or phrase and begin again.

6. At the end of 10 to 20 minutes open your eyes and resume your normal alert state.

✔✔Fantasy

This relaxation technique is based on the principle that whenever you vividly imagine an experience, you trigger the same physiological responses that would go along with the experience in real life. ''What the mind perceives, the mind believes.'' Therefore you want to imagine experiences that are calm and relaxing. Use as many senses as possible in your fantasy: sight, sound, smell, touch, taste. This will help trigger stronger physiological relaxation responses. This technique is frequently used by children to relieve pressure and anxiety. We call it daydreaming.

1. Pick a time and place in which you will not be disturbed.

2. Lie or sit in a comfortable position.

3. Close your eyes. Imagine yourself in a wonderful relaxing place. Weave in a creative, imaginative story full of wonderful experiences. Use as many senses as you can.

4. To get you started, choose from the following, or create your own.
   a. Take a walk on the beach, hear the surf, feel the warm sunlight, smell the ocean, look at the blue sky, taste salt spray...
   b. Go to the mountains, smell the pine trees, listen to the wind, walk with your lover, see the birds, feel the soft pine needles...
   c. Visit a mythical land, hear the song of the muses, see the castles glistening in the moonlight, smell the fragrant blossoms, taste the sweet fruits, touch the velvet garments...
   d. Float on a cloud, look down at the earth, smell...
   e. Imagine yourself conducting an orchestra...
   f. Create your own...

✓✓Counting Backward

Remember when you were told to fall asleep by counting sheep? And if you were still awake to count them backward? Well, there is wisdom in the folkways. Counting your breaths can help you relax, and it's also helpful for centering yourself when your mind is spinning with ideas or worries.

1. Pick a time and place in which you will not be disturbed.

2. Lie or sit in a comfortable position.

3. Close your eyes. Begin counting down, starting with 50, 75 or 100, depending on how long you wish to spend on this activity.

4. Count each breath you exhale. However, notice that you do not have to inhale immediately. You may rest comfortably for several seconds (up to 20 seconds for some people before inhaling).

5. If you should lose track of the number you are counting, don't worry. Just begin counting backward from the last number you remember.

6. When you have finished your countdown, either return to your normal alert state or switch to another relaxation activity.

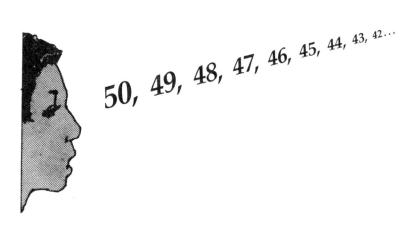

50, 49, 48, 47, 46, 45, 44, 43, 42...

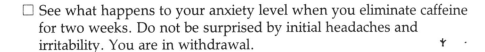

THE ROLE OF EXERCISE AND NUTRITION

Several other factors make a significant contribution in clearing your body. Their importance in overcoming anxiety cannot be stressed enough.

1. **A well-balanced diet.** While this will not eliminate stress or anxiety, it is one of your body's best defenses against stress and anxiety, especially if you have a highly reactive body or nervous system. The emphasis here is on a nutritious, well-balanced diet. Do not resort to fads or fancy diet plans. A healthy diet contributes significantly to:

    - Increasing physical endurance

    - Resisting disease

    - Increasing emotional stability

    Watch your tendency to use junk foods such as candy, chocolate and salty snacks for soothing during anxious times. These are not effective copers. In fact they frequently contribute to your symptoms.

    And watch out for alcohol, cigarettes and caffeine. Cigarettes contain more than 2,700 chemicals and are as effective for stuffing feelings as are drugs and alcohol. *Caffeine is a stimulant and mood altering drug.* As few as four cups of coffee a day have been shown to create panic attacks in some people. Under stress your body is more susceptible to stimulants. Read the labels on soft drinks, candy, medication and prepared foods. (And yes, unfortunately, chocolate does contain caffeine.)

    ☐ See what happens to your anxiety level when you eliminate caffeine for two weeks. Do not be surprised by initial headaches and irritability. You are in withdrawal.

THE ROLE OF EXERCISE
AND NUTRITION (continued)

2. **Exercise.** This is your body's best response to the fight/flight mechanism. In activating this mechanism, your body was originally preparing to exercise itself through fighting or fleeing. Hormones (adrenalin) and biochemicals (endorphins) are released into your body as part of your Emergency-Response System. When not used up by the physical exertion of fighting or fleeing, they remain in your system. This creates a chemical imbalance, mood changes and ultimately contributes to maintaining your Anxiety-Response-System.

Aerobic exercise provides substitute fight or flight responses. Choose from any of the following:

- Running

- Walking briskly

- Swimming

- Aerobic dance

- Bicycling

Choose any exercise that actively involves your large muscle groups. Your goal is to increase and sustain your pulse rate for 30 minutes three times per week. This is an excellent method for helping your body overcome anxiety. (And it will do wonders for your weight maintenance.)

Before starting any exercise program or dramatically changing your current one, it is best to check with your physician. This is particularly important if you have age, health or physical restrictions.

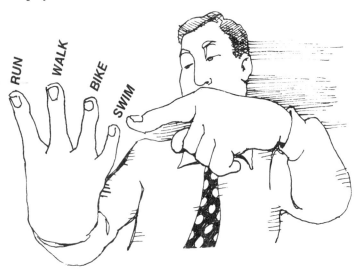

P A R T

III

Managing Your Life

MANAGING YOUR LIFE

This section is designed to help you develop skills and techniques for better managing your life. Remember that overcoming anxiety is a lifelong process. No one is forever anxiety-free. However, some persons have better management of their anxiety because they have practiced and mastered several basic techniques that work for them. You have already been exposed to several of these techniques. They will become skills for you as you practice and master them. Be aware that not all techniques are appropriate for all people at all times. But the more alternatives you have at your disposal, the greater your opportunity to manage the anxiety in your life.

In the last two units you have learned several concepts and skills for overcoming anxiety. Put a check by those skills you have already practiced:

- ☐ Recognizing the five subsystems affecting anxiety.
- ☐ Understanding automatic thoughts or images.
- ☐ Knowing the difference between anxiety, fear, phobia, panic.
- ☐ Identifying your five F's—fight, flee, freeze, fling, faint.
- ☐ Recognizing how anxiety helps and hurts you.
- ☐ Understanding the difference between behavior and emotions.
- ☐ Understanding the Emergency-Response System.
- ☐ Understanding the Anxiety-Response System.
- ☐ Identifying your anxiety-prone areas.
- ☐ Recognizing the role of hyperventilation in your anxiety.
- ☐ Using Relaxed Diaphragmatic Breathing.
- ☐ Utilizing four relaxation techniques: progressive relaxation, focus, fantasy, counting backwards.
- ☐ Maintaining a sensible, well-balanced diet.
- ☐ Exercising aerobically three times per week.

The rest of this book is dedicated to enlarging your choice of skills. "Try on" the different techniques. Spend some time developing mastery. Then see how they fit for you.

BUILDING AWARENESS

The first step in the management of any problem is becoming aware.

- Are you aware of circumstances that trigger your anxiety?
- Are you aware of your automatic thoughts?

Avoiding thinking about or facing your fear (which underlies anxiety) does not allow you to develop your awareness. "It" doesn't make you anxious, you do. Answering "*Why* am I anxious" doesn't give you clues as to what to do instead. If you are like most people, we are most aware of the least anxiety-provoking situations initially and can evoke the most immediate of our automatic thoughts. Later on, as the experience of anxiety becomes relatively more comfortable, we become more aware of other anxieties and deeper automatic thoughts.

Name a circumstance about which you feel anxious: _____

Now answer "*How*" am I making myself anxious? _____

_____

_____

Design a plan to approach what you fear: _____

_____

_____

Principle: When you create awareness about your anxiety and ask yourself how you are creating it for yourself, you give yourself power or control to do something about it.

Principle: Avoiding your fear or anxiety does not allow you an opportunity to evaluate and overcome it.

Use the form on the opposite page to help you build awareness of several areas of anxiety you wish to overcome.

Record the automatic thoughts (and images) about your anxiety as you become aware of them.

Then evaluate how your automatic thoughts are contributing to your anxiety. Finally, determine a plan for approaching your fear so that you may become more aware of deeper thoughts and images.

ANXIETY RECORD

Name a circumstance about which you feel anxious: _____
_____

Record your automatic thoughts: _____
_____
_____
_____
_____

Now answer *"How"* am I making myself anxious? _____
_____
_____
_____
_____

Design a plan to approach what you fear: _____
_____
_____
_____
_____

Implement your plan. Now what do you know about your anxiety? What new thoughts are you aware of?
_____
_____
_____
_____
_____

ANXIETY RECORD (continued)

Name a circumstance about which you feel anxious: _____
_____

Record your automatic thoughts: _____
_____
_____
_____
_____

Now answer "*How*" am I making myself anxious? _____
_____
_____
_____
_____

Design a plan to approach what you fear: _____
_____
_____
_____
_____

Implement your plan. Now what do you know about your anxiety? What new thoughts are you aware of?
_____
_____
_____
_____
_____

EXERCISE—AUTOMATIC THOUGHTS vs. COGNITIVE SUBSYSTEM

Now compare your automatic thoughts against the cognitive subsystem malfunctions. Put a check beside any malfunctions you recognize:

✓✓Cognitive System Malfunctions Checklist

☐ *Should/Must Thinking.* Changing decisions or preferences into rigid rules through the use of shoulds and musts.

☐ *All-Or-Nothing Thinking:* Judging events or persons in terms of dichotomous, black-or-white categories.

☐ *Overgeneralization:* Deciding that a single negative event is a forever occurrence.

☐ *Labeling:* A specific form of overgeneralization in which you give yourself a simplistic, usually negative label.

☐ *Binocular Thinking:* Magnifying your own flaws and errors while minimizing someone else's faults or creating mental catastrophe for yourself and exaggerating someone else's achievement.

☐ *Mind Reading:* A belief that you know what the other person is thinking or feeling without checking it out with them.

☐ *Fortune Telling:* Anticipating a negative outcome and then acting as if it has already occurred. Confusing the *possible* with the *probable* is the core of fortune telling.

☐ *Using Experts:* Accepting another person's opinion or advice as absolute without checking to see if they are qualified to make such a statement.

☐ *Emotional Reasoning:* Using your feelings as proof that something is so.

☐ *Personalization:* Assuming responsibility for a negative event when there is no basis for your guilt, or confusing *influence* with *control*.

To correct your Cognitive Subsystem Malfunctions, you must begin to "talk back," or rebut, the malfunction thinking. This is a valuable form of self-talk. It is very much like the control tower operator who "talks through" the landing process for an airplane pilot who has lost his airplane control panel. Parents will frequently help a child through a new or difficult experience by talking them through it. So do coaches. So will you, to help yourself overcome your anxiety. You become your own coach.

You have already begun the process by becoming more aware, identifying your automatic throughts and the Cognitive Subsystem Malfunctions they reveal. Now you will learn to rebut your malfunctions.

REBUT YOUR MALFUNCTIONS

RULES FOR REBUTTAL

1. **Rebuttals must be strong:** Overcoming years of cognitive malfunction requires that you make a strong stand. You may choose to use a strong, forceful voice to yourself or even make a shocking statement. ''STOP IT! You are OK!'' is a good strong rebuttal. Sometimes a physical act like snapping your fingers or pinching yourself can interrupt your train of thought.

2. **Rebuttals must be nonjudgmental:** Do not decide you are good or bad, right or wrong, should or shouldn't act or think a certain way. Be sure to be very exact in describing what is happening without making it bigger or less than it is. For example, you are not ''a wimp,'' you need some time for reflection.

3. **Rebuttals must be specific:** Make the problem specific. Examine the facts. State your rebuttal in terms of specific behavior. Check what is known for sure and use that in your rebuttal statements. For example, while your boss has not yet responded to your proposal, three days have passed, he has been out of town for two, his usual response time is four days. Assuming he has once again negated you is fantasy.

4. **Rebuttals must be balanced:** Offset the negative by including the positive in your rebuttal. For example, three persons declined your invitation to dance at the company party. Eight accepted. You are an acceptable dance partner.

Remember to keep these four rules in mind as you move to the next skill. These rules form the foundation for all your rebuttals.

✔✔The Three-Column Technique

You are now ready to combine three essential ingredients to overcome your anxiety. This technique, called the Three-Column Technique, is one of the most valuable tools you can utilize. It will serve you over and over again throughout your lifetime. Take the time to use it whenever you are feeling extremely anxious. It is particularly effective following a session in which you have used one of the relaxation techniques to help quiet your body and your mind.

To use the Three Column Technique you will:

- State the circumstance surrounding your anxiety.
- Put your automatic thoughts/images in the first column (use the previous exercises to help yourself identify them if necessary).
- Identify the Cognitive Subsystem Malfunctions each contains.
- Write a rebuttal to each of the malfunctions for each thought. Remember to follow the rules for rebuttal:
    Strong
    Nonjudgmental
    Specific
    Balanced

Practice using the Three-Column Technique form on page 56.

✔✔Reframing Technique

To overcome your anxiety about being physically or emotionally vulnerable, you can clear your mind. You do this by changing your cognitive set. Reframing is a specific form of rebuttal to your cognitive set. Your cognitive set is revealed by the thoughts and images you have. And it can be changed by reframing (changing) those thoughts and images.

Reframing is a mental way of choosing where to put the frame on the panorama that is your life. Since you cannot encompass all of it in the frame, you must pick that part which you choose to focus on. Where you focus determines your perceptions and your cognitive set. For example, if you were looking at a horse standing at a rose fence in a pasture with hills in the background, where you placed the frame in that panorama would determine what type of picture you saw. Placing the frame at the front of the horse gives a pictures of a horse's head and roses. Placing the frame at the horse's end gives a picture of a horse's tail and you know what else! So it is with life and anxiety.

Use the Reframing Exercise form on page 57.

THREE-COLUMN TECHNIQUE FORM

Circumstance _____

_____

Automatic Thought	Malfunction	Rebuttal Statement/Action
_____	_____	_____
_____	_____	_____
_____	_____	_____
_____	_____	_____
_____	_____	_____
_____	_____	_____
_____	_____	_____
_____	_____	_____
_____	_____	_____
_____	_____	_____
_____	_____	_____
_____	_____	_____
_____	_____	_____
_____	_____	_____
_____	_____	_____
_____	_____	_____
_____	_____	_____
_____	_____	_____
_____	_____	_____
_____	_____	_____
_____	_____	_____
_____	_____	_____
_____	_____	_____
_____	_____	_____

REFRAMING EXERCISE

Use the following exercise to practice reframing your cognitive set. Choose overall pictures in which you feel anxious or show signs of anxiety.

The overall picture	**The current frame**	**Reframed**
Low-level job, big organization	*Boring, useless, I hate work*	*Opportunity for advancement "I'll learn & prove myself."*

✔✔Challenge Yourself

Very often, when your life seems controlled by anxiety, it is difficult to take the time and energy to stop and challenge yourself and your beliefs. But challenge is a critical tool in managing your anxiety. Your anxiety can be about getting a raise, being promoted, being transferred, getting reassigned, being invited to speak, losing your family, acting silly, wearing the wrong clothes or any of a million other things. No matter what, you need to ask yourself, "What's the evidence?" for continuing to believe or behave in a way that's creating anxiety for yourself. Double check your thoughts and actions. Really *prove* your case to yourself, then cross-examine the evidence. Use the following questions to help challenge yourself:

My anxiety is: _____

- What evidence supports this idea? _____
  _____

- What evidence goes against this idea? _____
  _____

- Show me the logic: _____
  _____

- Is there really a cause and effect connection? How? _____
  _____

- Is this thought based in reality or in habitually thinking this thought?
  _____

- Am I accurate or exaggerating? _____
  _____

- Am I looking at it in all-or-nothing terms? _____
  _____

- Is my information source reliable? _____
  _____

- Am I confusing possibilities with probabilities? _____
  _____

- Am I judging on my feelings or on facts? _____
  _____

- What else do I need to know? _____
  _____

Challenging yourself is a skill that you can use whenever your mind is racing and your anxiety mounting. If you find that you cannot slow down enough to focus on the above questions, then merely *count your automatic thoughts*. When you can, jot those thoughts down. After you have several automatic thoughts written down, go back and challenge yourself on them.

✔✔Automatic Thought Log

_____

_____

_____

_____

_____

_____

_____

_____

_____

_____

_____

_____

_____

_____

_____

_____

_____

_____

_____

_____

_____

_____

_____

_____

✔✔Take Another Point of View

Have you noticed that when you are upset and anxious, you sometimes lose your perspective? It happens frequently. The unpleasant emotions and sensations surrounding an anxiety-producing situation sometimes cloud our thinking. We forget to look for alternatives, see solutions, understand another point of view or take the pressure off ourselves. We get muddled and see ourselves as the center of the universe, sure that all eyes in the room are on us as we arrive late at a conference or ask a question. Of course, this only serves to heighten our unpleasant emotions and sensations, further increasing our anxiety.

Learning to take another point of view is a skill you'll want to master as an aid to overcoming anxiety. You can do this by:

- ☐ Brainstorming other interpretations of the situation
- ☐ Keeping track of malfunctional thoughts
- ☐ Removing yourself from the center of focus
- ☐ Taking a broader point of view, e.g., from the top of a mountain
- ☐ Recognizing the limits of your control over the outcome

Jerri Jones was extremely afraid of being fired. If her supervisor didn't speak to her or acted distant, she immediately thought, "He's going to fire me, that's why he's being so cool." What other explanations could there be for the supervisor's aloofness?

1. _____

2. _____

3. _____

You might have responded that the supervisor was feeling ill that day, was preoccupied with a production problem, was generally aloof to all people, chose not to socialize with others, hired and fired on competence not friendship or many other alternatives. Do any of those support Jerri's expectation of being fired? Does she need to remain anxious because of the supervisor's behavior?

Now relate this technique to your own situation:

Situation	Automatic Thought	Alternative Theories

✔✔The So-What Technique

When you feel anxious there's a tendency for your thoughts to race into the future, predicting the most horrible of outcomes. The "so-what" technique is a tool to use to master the tendency to create catastrophe before it occurs. (Remember, if it occurs you will be so busy handling it that you won't have time to feel anxious!)

Underlying the problem of making dire predictions is your fear (vulnerability) that you will not be able to handle a difficult situation. You forget to assess the odds that it will happen and lose sight of your past track record. Remember to ask yourself **"How many of my past predictions of doom and gloom actually came true in their entirety?"**

You can also lose sight of the resources you do possess for coping—which is part of your feeling of vulnerability. Don't get hung up on mastering bad situations, all you want to do is cope. Ask yourself **"What resources and strategies do I already have for coping with this?"** *Make a list of them, write them down for future reference.* (Remember to include the techniques and strategies you have already learned in this book.)

Finally, you need to remind yourself that *you can't always control the outcome of a situation, but you can control your response to it*. To help yourself accomplish this, begin to ask **"So what if it happens? Then what can I do? And then what will happen? So what if it happens? Then what can I do? And then what will happen? So what if it happens? Then what can I do...."**

THE "SO-WHAT" EXERCISE (continued)

By doing the following "so-what" exercise, you will soon discover you have many ways of coping, you have resources to draw upon and you can accept and cope with the worst possible outcome. So why worry?

"SO-WHAT" EXERCISE

I fear that this will happen: _____

So what if it happens? _____

Then what can I do? _____

And then what will happen? _____

So what if it happens? _____

Then what can I do? _____

And then what will happen? _____

So what if it happens? _____

Then what can I do? _____

And then what will happen? _____

So what if it happens? _____

Then what can I do? _____

And then what will happen? _____

So what if it happens? _____

Then what can I do? _____

And then what will happen? _____

So what if it happens? _____

Then what can I do? _____

And then what will happen? _____

IMAGERY

Many of the exercises and techniques already discussed have been aimed at helping change the way you *think* about your anxiety. There are several techniques to help you *see* and *act* differently. See how many of these are useful to you in overcoming your anxiety.

You may be asking, "How can I possibly *see* my anxiety?" Studies have shown that people do, in fact, see, or visualize, events that produce anxiety. In the first chapter, we discussed automatic thoughts or *images* that accompany, and in fact precipitate, anxiety. The following exercises are aimed at helping you use your visualization skills or imagery to overcome anxiety. But first, you must become aware of the kind of imagery involved in anxiety.

Think about the circumstances that surround your anxiety. Close your eyes. What do you see? Another way to tap into this is to daydream or recall daydreams. As you think about an image or daydream, ask yourself the following questions:

- What is the picture I see?
- How would I describe it?
- Is it in color? What colors?
- Is there sound?
- Is there movement?
- Do I smell anything?
- Do I hear anything?
- Are there feelings or sensations?

Just as you learned that you could modify or change your malfunctional thinking, you can also modify and change your malfunctional images. You can do this by using the Turn-off Technique, Repetition, Time Projection, and TV-Set Technique.

✔✔Turn-Off Technique

A bus driver was involved in a bus-car accident. For months afterward, images of the accident kept cropping up in his mind. Using the Turn-off Technique allowed him to focus once again on his driving and return safely to work. This technique is especially useful if you also find yourself reliving a particularly awful experience.

The purpose of this technique is to "turn off" the automatic image or fantasy by interrupting it with something else. You can clap your hands, whistle to yourself, or snap your fingers. What other interrupters can you think of? Write them down.

_____

_____

_____

To practice the Turn-off Technique, bring the disturbing image to mind on purpose. Now interrupt it. Did the image disappear? Do this exercise again. Keep practicing until you can make the image disappear. It is sometimes very useful to visualize a pleasant image as soon as the unpleasant one has disappeared.

✔✔Repetition Technique

By repeating in full an unpleasant daydream or fantasy you can gradually incorporate changes to bring it into line with a more pleasant reality. You must make a conscious effort to do this. Otherwise you will merely continue to repeat the unpleasant fantasy and continue to feel anxious about anticipated events or outcomes.

✔✔Time Projection Technique

This technique is especially useful when you are anxiously *anticipating* a speech, presentation or event.

Jane Eyer had just become the first woman vice president of sales and marketing in her large midwest company. Three hundred twenty-five sales representatives from around the country would be waiting to see how well she presented the new product line at the national sales meeting. Jane had the jitters! She just couldn't allow herself to make any mistakes. This was a make-or-break speech. Two weeks ahead she already was feeling nauseated. Her administrative assistant needed adequate lead time to get the slides and visual aides ready. Jane couldn't focus on her presentation. The mere thought of it made her feel ill. What could she do?

Jane could use Time Projection to manage her anxiety. She should:
- Visualize herself at the event.
- See herself performing as she desires. Watch her actions, speech, behavior.
- See the people responding well to her.
- See the positive consequences and outcomes of her behavior.
- Project herself three months, six months, a year into the future.
- See the positive outcomes.

The time projection technique is the one used by star athletes who use visualization to improve their performance. If it works for them, it can work for you.

✔✔TV-Set Technique

By gaining management of your imagery, you can gain management of your anxiety. You may have heard the saying, "What the mind perceives, the mind believes." Research has shown that the brain does not differentiate between imagined images and images that come from perception of the outside world (reality). Therefore, by controlling the images that your brain creates, you also control your perception.

Think of your mind images as the ones you see on a TV set. If you don't like the image you see, change the channel, tune it in, tune it out.

A variation of this is to become the producer and director of the TV soap opera of your life. You write the script, direct the actors and modify any scenes that are not to your liking.

Visualization is a very powerful tool. It can be used by sales people to make their sales quotas a reality. It is a way to achieve goals. And it is a way to overcome your anxiety.

A FINAL ROUND

So far we have discussed ways to overcome your anxiety by using cognitive techniques, relaxation techniques and imagery techniques. There are several more general strategies to add to your arsenal. They include:

- Coping self-statements
- Redirection
- Breathers
- Relaxation
- Play
- Humor
- Routines
- Spiritual and emotional support

✔✔Coping Self-Statements

When you were young your parent or teacher was frequently there to reassure you and calm you when you were upset. Today, you have to give that reassurance and soothing to yourself. It is especially important to utilize these reassuring and soothing statements when you are feeling vulnerable and anxious. Unfortunately, too often that is the time when we forget them. In fact, during these times our negative self-talk becomes far stronger than our coping self-talk. Therefore, many people like to put coping self-statements, often called affirmations, on the mirror to remind themselves of their assets and competencies daily. Another method is to make lists of coping self-statements that you can refer to as needed.

SELF-STATEMENTS

Follow these examples to create statements that are meaningful for you:

☐ To *prepare* myself for an anxiety-producing situation I can say:
"I'll be OK. I've done this before."
"Take things one at a time, there's a solution."
"Once I get started it always gets easier. Let's begin."
"I'm doing this because I choose to, so it's OK."
"It's OK for me to feel anxious, I know I'll be OK."

_____

_____

_____

☐ To *confront and handle* a situation I can say:
"Stay focused on the task, you'll do it."
"I can use my breathing skills to handle this."
"This doesn't have to be perfect, just done."
"Take it easy and slowly."

_____

_____

_____

☐ To cope with feeling *overwhelmed* I can say:
"This is just anxiety, not death."
"These feeling don't stop me, I can continue even though I'm uncomfortable."
"This will pass soon, and in the meantime I will keep functioning."
"This is just my body reacting, I have skills to cope with it."

_____

_____

_____

☐ To *reinforce* my success in handling my anxiety I can say:
"Congratulations, I did it!"
"Yes, I'm proud I faced myself."
"One more bit of evidence I can handle this."
"Even though I was anxious, I used my skills and was able to do it."

_____

_____

_____

✔✔Redirection Techniques

Redirection is a common technique that you are probably already using without knowing it. Another word for this technique is distraction. Anyone with children knows that it is easier to get two-year olds to give up a toy by distracting them with another more appealing toy. It works much better than trying to get them to give up the toy they have by asking for it or taking it away from them. So it is with redirection. You shift your attention to something more positive (or even neutral) rather than trying to shift *away* from something negative. (Remember the results of telling yourself not to think about pink elephants). You can redirect by:

- *Externalization*—focus your attention on sensations outside your body. You can do this by *observing carefully* what you see around you; *listening carefully* to background noises, random conversations; *feeling textures* of clothing, paper, upholstery or things around you; *tasting or smelling* the elements of your surrounding environment; *doing repetitive tasks* like counting ceiling tiles or tapping your finger repetitively.

- *Concentrating on simple tasks* like balancing your checkbook or recalling words of a poem or song.

- *Conversation*—talking to a friend or even a stranger in an active manner will distract your attention from your anxiety as long as you don't talk about the situation that is generating the anxiety.

- *Work*—more people use work to distract from anxiety than are aware of it. Cleaning the cabinets, straightening the garage, organizing your desk all have the beneficial task of distracting you from your anxiety and getting something accomplished at the same time. However, a word of caution: becoming a workaholic is no more effective in coping with anxiety than is becoming an alcoholic.

- *Play*—finding an activity that holds your interest and is pleasurable is an excellent form of redirection. That activity can vary from working crossword puzzles to engaging in a game of tennis.

✔✔Breathers

Very often, anxiety-prone people tend to jump from one activity right into another without taking a break. Taking the time to unwind between activities is critical for reducing anxiety. What you choose to do to unwind can be almost anything that works for you: reading a book, jogging, daydreaming or talking with friends. The important thing is to give yourself a breather, even just a 10-minute snooze, between activities. A word of caution: use of such substances as alcohol, cigarettes or ''recreational'' drugs are poor choices, for in spite of their popularity for this purpose, they ultimately just create *more* anxiety.

✔✔Relaxation

In the previous chapters, you learned several relaxation techniques. There are many more to choose from. Some forms of relaxation are active while others are passive. Either way, the purpose of relaxation is to help you feel more refreshed and at ease.

Put an X by those relaxation techniques you use. Put a check by those you wish to learn:

Passive
- ☐ Biofeedback
- ☐ Hot tubs, showers, baths
- ☐ Massage and body work
- ☐ Meditation or prayer
- ☐ Movies and theater
- ☐ Music
- ☐ Reading
- ☐ Self-hypnosis
- ☐ Sleep
- ☐ Television
- ☐ Yoga

Active
- ☐ Hobby classes
- ☐ Dancing
- ☐ Crafts and hobbies
- ☐ Individual sports
- ☐ Time with friends
- ☐ Exercise
- ☐ Trips and vacations
- ☐ Shopping
- ☐ Team sports
- ☐ Games
- ☐ Walks and hikes

70

✔✔Play

Play is not just for children. It is essential for good health and anxiety management. Play includes anything that is entertaining and fun. Many of the activities that are included in relaxation can be considered play. Additionally, romping with your kids, giggling with friends, joshing with an old friend are wonderful forms of play. Including "play in your day" reduces your physical and emotional stress, improves your sense of humor and increases your tolerance for anxiety.

✔✔Humor

Seeing the paradox of a situation, taking a different perspective, keeping things in proportion are all contributors to a sense of humor. They are also contributors to overcoming anxiety. Whenever you begin to take yourself or a situation so seriously that you begin to feel anxious, step back and find something humorous about it. The humor will refresh your perspective and bring your anxiety under control. Research has shown that laughter helps release anxiety controlling hormones into your system. So, whatever it is that's bothering you, step back, look at it from the viewpoint of a TV sitcom writer and let yourself laugh.

✔✔Spiritual and Emotional Support

The root of anxiety is feeling vulnerable. The presence of emotional and spiritual support is a significant contributor to reducing that sense of vulnerability. The presence of close, caring persons with whom you can share concerns is of immeasurable value. Often the need for approval and the need to please others gets in the way of reaching out for assistance and care. It can also get in the way of giving assistance and care. Check yourself. Are you giving and receiving support from loved ones?

Spiritual support is what gives you a sense of meaning in the world. It does not necessarily mean religion, although for many persons it is one and the same. However, spirituality allows you to put events within a larger context. People with a sense of deep spiritual support feel a sense of serenity and strength. They turn to it for help in overcoming obstacles and confusion. If you have questions about your spiritual support, now might be a good time to explore your spirituality. It is an invaluable source in coping with anxiety.

✔✔Traditions and Routines

You are probably extremely busy living your life. Anxiety can be extremely disruptive to you. Yet, the techniques you have learned throughout this book do not happen by chance. You use them because you have taken the time and energy to develop and practice them. Now you need to build them into your daily life. Take the time to make relaxation and play a regular part of your day. Set aside time to practice and perfect any skills that you feel will be useful to you in overcoming anxiety. Establish a schedule for yourself that allows you time for coping in chaos. Recognize the value of traditions and routines for giving continuity to your life.

PART

IV

Final Review

FINAL REVIEW

This book has given you a general understanding of anxiety and techniques to use to overcome it. Take the time right now to review the skills and techniques you have learned. Put a check by any skills you want to review and improve:

NOTES

NOTES

NOTES

NOTES

OVER 150 BOOKS AND 35 VIDEOS AVAILABLE IN THE 50-MINUTE SERIES

We hope you enjoyed this book. If so, we have good news for you. This title is part of the best-selling *50-MINUTE™ Series* of books. All *Series* books are similar in size and identical in price. Many are supported with training videos.

To order *50-MINUTE* Books and Videos or request a free catalog, contact your local distributor or Crisp Publications, Inc., 1200 Hamilton Court, Menlo Park, CA 94025. Our toll-free number is (800) 442-7477.

50-Minute Series Books and Videos Subject Areas . . .

Management
Training
Human Resources
Customer Service and Sales Training
Communications
Small Business and Financial Planning
Creativity
Personal Development
Wellness
Adult Literacy and Learning
Career, Retirement and Life Planning

Other titles available from Crisp Publications in these categories

Crisp Computer Series
The Crisp Small Business & Entrepreneurship Series
Quick Read Series
Management
Personal Development
Retirement Planning